The Kite

The Kite

Written by Mary Packard

Illustrated by Benrei Huang

My First READER

children's press®

A Division of Scholastic Inc.

New York Toronto London Auckland Sydney
Mexico City New Delhi Hong Kong
Danbury, Connecticut

Library of Congress Cataloging-in-Publication Data

Packard, Mary.
  The kite / written by Mary Packard ; illustrated by Benrei Huang.–
1st American ed.
      p. cm. – (My first reader)
Summary: A child watches his kite fly high in the sky.
  ISBN 0-516-22930-3 (lib. bdg.)   0-516-24632-1 (pbk.)
  [1. Kites–Fiction.] I. Huang, Benrei, ill. II. Title. III. Series.
  PZ7.P1247Ki 2003
  [E]–dc21
                                    2003003690

Note to Parents and Teachers

Once a reader can recognize and identify the 20 words
used to tell this story, he or she will be able to read successfully the
entire book. These 20 words are repeated throughout the story, so that
young readers will be able to easily recognize
the words and understand their meaning.

The 20 words used in this book are:

birds	my
clouds	on
could	ride
fly	see
high	sky
I	so
if	the
in	touch
it	trees
kite	will

See my kite.

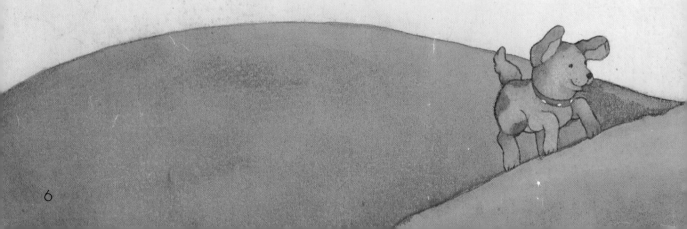

See it fly, fly, fly.

9

See it fly so high?

See it fly in the sky.

Will it touch the trees?

14

Will it touch the birds?

17

Will it touch the clouds?

Will it touch the sky?

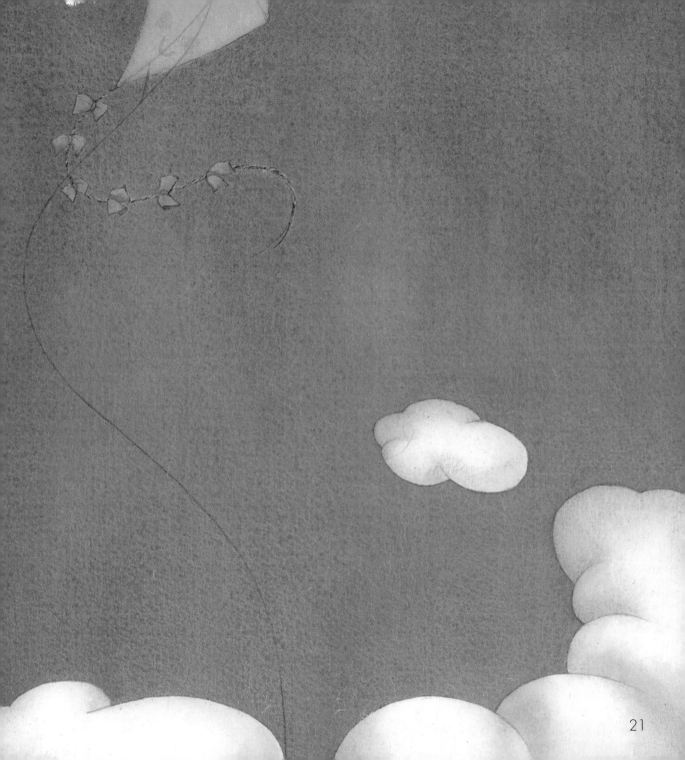

See my kite.

See it fly so high.

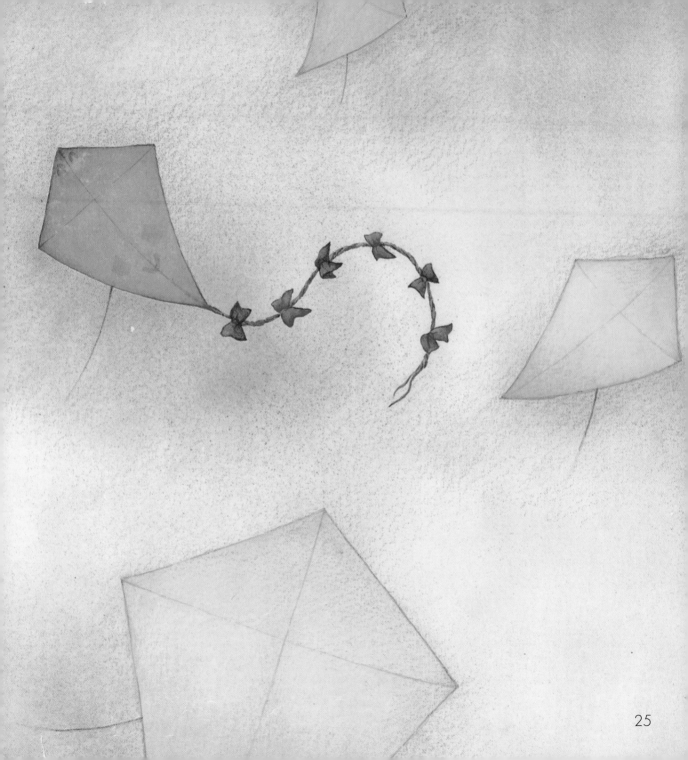

If I could ride on my kite,

I could fly, fly, fly.

ABOUT THE AUTHOR

Mary Packard has been writing children's books for as long as she can remember. Packard lives in Northport, New York, with her family. Besides writing, she loves music, theater, animals, and, of course, children of all ages.

ABOUT THE ILLUSTRATOR

Benrei Huang received her master's in illustration from the School of Visual Arts. She has illustrated more than thirty children's books. Huang lives in New York City with her husband and young son.

10-03

ER   Packard, Mary
       The kite.

GAYLORD RG